The Schemha Magick

By Lightworker

Printed in the USA

ISBN: 978-0-557-09241-3

Table of Contents

Introduction

Caveat

This text deals with astral and physical forces that can be dangerous if misused or used carelessly. It is important that the reader know his or her own physical, emotional, and psychological limits before undertaking the studies within this book. The exercises herein and techniques discussed are not to be used in lieu of the services of trained and qualified professionals such as physicians or psychologists. The reader is responsible, in every way, for his or her actions involved in using the rituals in this book and the author, publisher and the distributor of this text are not responsible for any undesirable outcomes from the use of this book.

List of Books by the Author

To buy more of the Author's books please go to
www.Lightworker.biz
Available in print and download versions.

Magickal Evocation Rituals
Luciferian Magick
The Necronomicon Ritual Book
Astrology Magick
Numerology Magick
Tarot Magick
Rune Magick
And over 70 more…

Introduction

This Schemhamephorash Angel's book is the most powerful and yet simple Magick you will ever do! You only need a candle, bell, rope and incense and 10 minutes to do each ritual. After thousands of years and endless hard to understand Grimoire Magick books on the subject, this book, The Schemhamephorash Angels, finally reveals the true secrets of the Schemhamephorash! In chapter 1, The Schemhamephorash Angel Evocation Ritual shows you step by step how to easily summon these 72 Angels of the Schemhamephorash to visible appearance! And in chapter 2 there is a list of all the Schemhamephorash Angels with an easy to understand description for each Angel so you can easily summon them for money, health, love, psychic abilities and many more things as well. Chapter 3 is a Book of Shadows to record your rituals and results. Unlike spells which require a belief system, these evocation rituals don't require you to believe in them at all as these Schemhamephorash Angels are doing your bidding for you!

I. The Schemhamephorash Angel Evocation Ritual

The Angel's Sigil

The Schemhamephorash Angel Evocation Ritual

Temple Set Up

Put on Robe and wear Angel's Sigil as a necklace

Put cloth on altar, with bell, lit candle and sandalwood incense on it

Put rope circle around you and the altar and face East

Read description of Spirit and write Request

Opening Rituals

Ring Bell-*"this temple is now open"*

Opening Prayer: *"Before me is Raphael, behind me is Gabriel, on my right side is Michael and on my left side is Auriel. For around me shines the Pentagram and within me shines the six - rayed star"*

Spirit Communication

Stare at spirit's sigil and visualize your request

Say this 3 times: *"I summon and evoke thee, (name of spirit), to visibly appear before me and answer my request of (request).* To communicate with the spirit close your eyes and ask a question(s) and then say into the recorder what you **feel, hear, think** and **see** as your answer from the spirit.

Now Close your eyes and visualize request completed.

Closing Rituals

License to Depart: *"I thank thee, Angels, this ritual is now done. All forces, Entities and Energies shall go about their business until again I call. In the Ultimate Name, go in peace to do my bidding. Harm nobody and none and nothing that I have, that I like and love. So mote it be."*

Ring bell-*"this temple is now closed"*

Record in Book of Shadows.

End.

II. The Schemhamephorash Angels

Angel: Vehuaiah

Description: arts, sciences, military

Angel: Ieliel

Description: to obtain victory over attacker

Angel: Sitael

Description: nobility, magnanimity and great

works

Angel: Elemiah

Description: travel, maritime expeditions, useful discoveries

Angel: Mahasiah

Description: high sciences, occult philosophy,

theology, liberal arts

Angel: Lelahel

Description: knowledge, cure illness, love, and art

science, fortune

Angel: Achaiah

Description: patience, secrets of nature

Angel: Cahetel

Description: chases away evil spirits, agriculture

Angel: Haziel

Description: friendship, reconciliation

Angel: Aladiah

Description: rage, pestilence, cure of disease, good health, success in life

Angel: Lauviah

Description: influences great persons, the wise and those who become famous through their talents

Angel: Hahaiah

Description: influences thoughts, dreams and reveals hidden meanings to mortals, shows meaning of Occult symbols

Angel: Iezalel

Description: friendship, fidelity

Angel: Mebahel

Description: justice, truth, liberty

Angel: Hariel

Description: arts, sciences, influences discoveries and new methodologies

Angel: Hakamiah

Description: rules over crowded heads and great captains, influences fire and war

Angel: Lauviah

Description: high sciences, marvelous discoveries,

revelations in dreams

Angel: Caliel

Description: allows knowledge of truth in proceedings, allows innocence to triumph

Angel: Leuviah

Description: connects your prayers directly to God

Angel: Pahaliah

Description: rules theology and morals

Angel: Nelecael

Description: destroys evil spirits, astronomy, mathematics, geography and all abstract sciences, influences the wise

Angel: Ieiael

Description: fortune, diplomacy, commerce, influences voyages, discoveries, maritime expeditions, protects shipwrecks

Angel: Melahel

Description: serves against arms, safety in travel, rules water and plants of the earth

Angel: Hahuiah

Description: rules over exiles, fugitives, prisoners, protects against robbers and assassins

Angel: Nithhaiah

Description: occult sciences, revelations in dreams, and those who seek the truth and practice of Magick of the sages which is that of God

Angel: Haaiah

Description: protects those who seek the truth, rules over politicians, diplomats

Angel: Jerathel

Description: protects us against those who provoke us, rules over propagation of light, civilization and liberty

Angel: Seeiah

Description: heals illness, protects against fires, ruined buildings, collapse, maladies, rules over health and longevity

Angel: Reiiel

Description: rules over religious sentiment, divine philosophy and meditation

Angel: Omael

Description: multiplies species, influences chemists, doctors, surgeons

Angel: Lecabel

Description: rules over agriculture, astronomy, mathematics, geometry

Angel: Vasariah

Description: rules over justice, he influences magistrates, legal executives and attorneys

Angel: Iehuiah

Description: helps you overcome your dark side, your negative impulses

Angel: Lehahiah

Description: rules over crowed heads, princes and nobles

Angel: Chevakiah

Description: rules over testaments, successions and supports peace in families

Angel: Menadel

Description: invoked to retain one's employment

Angel: Aniel

Description: sciences, arts

Angel: Haamiah

Description: rules over religious occults and protects those who seek truth

Angel: Rehael

Description: health, longevity

Angel: Ieiazel

Description: rules over printing and libraries, he influences writers

Angel: Hahahel

Description: influences priests

Angel: Mikael

Description: rules over moarchs, princes and

nobles

Angel: Veuahiah

Description: rules over peace and influences

prosperity of empires

Angel: Ielahiah

Description: protects a magistrate and to win a

lawsuit

Angel: Sealiah

Description: vegetation and nature

Angel: Ariel

Description: helps discover hidden treasures, and

dreams

Angel: Asaliah

Description: rules over justice

Angel: Michael

Description: protects peace and union between married couples, friendship

Angel: Vehuel

Description: rules over great people who have distinguished themselves with their talents

Angel: Daniel

Description: rules over justice, attorneys, magistrates

Angel: Hahasiah

Description: chemistry, physics

Angel: Imamiah

Description: travel and those who seek the truth

Angel: Nanael

Description: high sciences, influences religious

men, teachers, magistrates

Angel: Nithael

Description: rules over emperors, kings, princes

Angel: Mabaiah

Description: rules over morality and religion

Angel: Poiel

Description: rules over fame and philosophy

Angel: Nemmamiah

Description: rules over captains, admirals, generals and those who fight in a just cause

Angel: Ieialel

Description: cures illnesses, and problems with the eyes, rules over fire, influences metal workers, and those involved in commerce

Angel: Harahel

Description: rules over treasures, archives, and all rare and precious closets, influences book printing and the book trade and all those involved in the business

Angel: Mizrael

Description: heals spiritual ills and delivers from those who persecute one, rules over artists

Angel: Umabel

Description: friendship, astronomy, physics, artists

Angel: Iahhel

Description: rules over philosophers, enlightened

ones

Angel: Anianuel

Description: protects against accidents, preserve

health and illness

Angel: Mehiel

Description: protects against ferocious animals, rules the wise, teachers and authors, influences printing and bookshops and all those in that business

Angel: Damabiah

Description: rules over seas, rivers, springs maritime expeditions and naval construction, sailors, pilots, fishing and all those in that business

Angel: Manakel

Description: vegetation and aquatic animals, sleep and dreams

Angel: Iaiel

Description: rules over change, preservation of
monuments and longevity

Angel: Chabuiah

Description: preserves health and cures diseases, agriculture, fertility

Angel: Rochel

Description: finds lost or hidden objects, fortune,

Angel: Iibamiam

Description: rules over generation of beings

Angel: Haiel

Description: protects those who request him, gives victory and peace, influences military and weapons

Angel: Mumiah

Description: sciences, medicine, physics, health, longevity.

III. Book of Shadows

Book of Shadows

Book of Shadows